PETS PLUS

Cats

Honor Head

A+

Smart Apple Media

Published by Smart Apple Media, an imprint of Black Rabbit Books
P.O. Box 3263, Mankato, Minnesota 56002
www.blackrabbitbooks.com

Printed in the United States of America at Corporate Graphics, Inc.
North Mankato, Minnesota.

Published by arrangement with the Watts Publishing Group LTD, London.

Library of Congress Cataloging-in-Publication Data
Head, Honor.
 Cats / Honor Head.
    p. cm. — (Pets plus)
 Includes index.
 Summary: "Describes behavioral characteristics of wild and domestic cats. Helps readers
 decide if a pet cat is right for them, and gives suggestions on caring for a pet cat"--Provided by publisher.
 ISBN 978-1-59920-698-1 (library binding)
 1. Cats—Juvenile literature. I. Title.
 SF445.7.H424 2013
 636.8--dc23

2011035939

Created by Taglines Creative Ltd: www.taglinescreative.com
Author: Honor Head
Consultant: Sally Morgan
Series designer: Hayley Cove
Editor: Jean Coppendale

Picture credits
t=top b=bottom l=left r=right m=middle
Cover: Lion cub, Shutterstock/Mike Rogal; kitten, Shutterstock/Fesus Robert
Intro pictures: kitten and cub, Shutterstock/Eric Isselee; p4t Arco Images/Alamy, 4b
Peck and Fernandez/Superstock; p5t Shutterstock/Sari O'Neal, 5b Shutterstock/ Elaine
Nash; p6 Shutterstock/Ruth Black; p7 Angela Hampton; p8t Shutterstock/ Medvedev
Andrey; 8b Shutterstock/Becky Stares; p9 Ardea/John Daniels; p10 Shutterstock/Krugloff;
p11t Shutterstock/Scantaur, 11b Shutterstock/Photolink; p12 Shutterstock/ Gemenacom;
p13 Shutterstock/Monkey Business Images; p14 Shutterstock/Zhuchkova
Olena; p15 Shutterstock/Ersler Dmitry; p16l Shutterstock/Stefanie van der
Vinden, 16r Shutterstock/Iceman J; p17t Shutterstock/B. Didukh, 17b
Shutterstock/Tompet; p18 Shutterstock/Villiers Steyn; p19 Lifecycle l-r
Shutterstock/Evgeny Dubinchuk, 26kot, 6493866629; 19b
Shutterstock/Larsek; p20t Shutterstock/Karamysh, 20b Shutterstock/
Andreas Doppelmayr; p21t Ardea/Christian Heinrich, 21b Shutterstock/
Steve Brigman; p22l Ardea/John Daniels, 22r Ardea/Tom and Pat Leeson;
p23l Ardea/Duncan Fisher, 23r Superstock/Agefotostock; p24t Ardea/Jean
Michel Labat, 24b Shutterstock/Melanie DeFazio; p25 Shutterstock/
Ivonne Wierink; p26l and r Shutterstock/Eric Isselee; p27
Shutterstock/Cheryle Ann Quigley

PO 1436 / Feb 2012

9 8 7 6 5 4 3 2 1

Contents

The meaning of the words in **bold** can be
found in the glossary.

Small Cats, Big Cats

Your cute and cuddly pet cat is part of the same family as wild cats, such as lions, tigers, and panthers.

Teeth and Claws

Pet cats and wild cats look very similar. They have large eyes, whiskers, sharp teeth, and claws. Both wild and pet cats can run fast and climb trees. They both use their senses of sight, smell, and hearing to hunt down **prey**.

▼ This black cat (top) looks like a small version of a wild panther (below).

Look Alike

Many pet cats have fur that is the same color and has the same markings as wild cats. A cat's fur helps to **camouflage** it in the wild and hide it from enemies.

▼ The Scottish wild cat (below) looks like a tabby cat (right), but it has a much bigger tail and a thicker coat.

From Wild to Pet

Small wild cats were **domesticated** in ancient Egypt. They helped to keep rats and mice away from the bags of grain in outbuildings. Gradually, the ancient Egyptians fed them and they became pets. But tame cats can turn wild very easily. If they are left to fend for themselves, they will become **feral** and behave like wild cats again.

Why a Cat?

Most cats enjoy being stroked and cared for. They can also be very playful and will make a great friend if they are treated properly.

Family Member

If you have a cat it will quickly become one of the family. Kittens and cats love to play and you can have lots of fun with them just running around with a piece of string or a ball of rolled up paper. Many people find stroking a cat very relaxing and soothing.

PET POINT

Cats, like any other pets, are not toys and should always be treated with respect.

▲ Most cats like to run and jump and will enjoy a game of chase.

Everyday Routine

Cats don't need to be taken for walks but they do need daily care. Cats need to be fed every day and brushed regularly. A kitten will need to be trained. Cats can be left alone during the day with enough food and water, but they should not be left alone overnight.

Not Always a Kitten

You may fall for a cute, fluffy kitten, but remember kittens grow into cats, and cats can live for up to 20 years. Vet bills can be expensive, and your pet will need to be taken care of if you go on vacation.

▼ All long-haired cats will need to be **groomed** every day with a pet comb or brush.

Which Cat?

There are many different types of cats.
Do you want a **purebred** cat or a **mixed breed**?
One with short hair or long hair?

Purebred or Mixed?

Purebred cats have parents of the
same **breed,** or type, so the kittens
look like their parents. Mixed breed
cats may not look like their parents
at all. Some purebred cats may need
a special diet or lots of grooming.
If there is a certain breed of cat that
you like, speak to a breeder to see
if it will suit your lifestyle.

▲ This Scottish fold is a purebred
cat. It gets its name from the way
its ears fold down.

▲ Mixed breed kittens in a **litter**
from the same mother may all look
very different.

Long or Short Hair?

Long-haired cats will need to be
combed or brushed every day.
If you don't do this, their fur
could get very matted and you
may have to take them to the vet.
If you have a busy family life, it's
best to choose a short-haired cat.

Rescue Cats

There are thousands of cats and kittens in **animal shelters** that are looking for homes. Shelters often have purebred as well as mixed breed cats. Experts at the shelter will give you advice on how to choose and care for your pet.

▼ Experts at the animal shelter will help you to find a pet that's right for you.

Your Pet's New Home

 It's the day you're going to pick up your new pet. You might be very excited, but your new pet may be scared and nervous.

Getting Ready

Before your new pet arrives, decide where it will eat, sleep, and use the **litter box**. Put the litter box and food bowls in a quiet place away from doors that are used a lot. Keep the litter box close to the food bowls, but not right next to them.

Quiet and Gentle

You should keep your pet indoors for the first few days. Speak to it quietly saying its name so that it gets to know you and the sound of your voice. Stroke it gently. If you have other pets, especially cats or dogs, keep them apart for a few days.

◀ Your pet will soon get to know you and trust you if you treat it gently.

▲ Your pet will find its own favorite places in the home.

Exploring the Home

For the first two or three days try to keep your pet in one or two rooms. This will give it a chance to get to know you. Then let your pet explore the rest of the house. Introduce your cat to any other pets you may have but don't leave them alone together until they are used to each other.

Do It!

Checklist: Things you will need for your new pet:

- Cat carrier
- Pet bed or box with a cushion or blanket
- Food
- Two bowls—one for water, one for food
- Old newspapers to put under food bowls and litter box
- Brush or comb for long-haired cat
- Litter box
- Bag of litter
- Cat flap

Caring for Your Cat

Your pet is trusting you to look after it. There are a few basic rules you should follow to keep it healthy and happy.

Meal Times

Try to feed your pet at the same time every day. A kitten should have about four small meals a day. A cat needs two meals, one in the morning and one in the evening. Make sure your pet always has a bowl of fresh water. Do not give your pet milk because this can make some cats sick.

▼ If you have more than one cat, make sure each pet has its own food bowl.

Toilet Time

If your pet uses a litter box, make sure that it is cleaned every day. When you clean the box wear plastic gloves and always wash your hands well afterwards.

Going Out

Your pet should be **microchipped** before it goes outside (see page 29) in case it gets lost or has an accident. All cats should be **neutered** when they are old enough to stop unwanted kittens. Male cats that are not neutered often have nasty fights with other male cats or wander away from home.

▼ A vet can trace a cat's owners quickly and easily if it has a microchip.

Handling Your Pet

Most kittens and cats will enjoy being picked up and stroked. If you are gentle, your pet will soon trust you to handle it.

Good Support

When you pick up your pet hold it under its bottom with one hand and support its body with the other hand. Do not squeeze it around the middle or leave its back legs dangling down. Never drop your pet. Always put it back down on the floor gently.

PET POINT
If your pet doesn't want to be picked up, leave it alone.

▶ Always lift your pet properly when you pick it up, and never run around while holding a cat.

▲ Your pet will love being stroked and gently scratched on the top of its head and behind its ears.

Tummy Tickle

Kittens and cats can get hurt very easily. Never chase or hit your pet, grab its tail, or pull its whiskers. Your pet may enjoy having its head and ears rubbed and its chin tickled. Some cats enjoy a tummy tickle but not all of them do. If your pet doesn't like it, don't do it.

Watch Those Claws

A kitten or cat will automatically use its sharp claws if it is playing, so make sure you keep your hands out of the way. If your cat scratches you, don't scream, and never hit it. Say a firm "no" and turn away. Wash the scratch in warm water with some disinfectant.

Wild Cousins

Cats have been domesticated for thousands of years, but your pet and wild cats will still often behave in the same way.

Keeping Clean

Pet and wild cats spend a lot of time licking themselves to keep their fur smooth and clean, especially after eating. Cats have a very rough tongue that stops their fur from becoming matted and cleans away dirt. A smooth, clean coat will make sure both wild and pet cats stay healthy.

▲ Cats have a rough tongue like sandpaper. This cheetah (left) and calico pet cat (right) are both licking their fur clean.

Wild Ways

Cats in the wild spend a lot of their time hunting for food. Some pet cats hunt small animals such as mice but may not eat them. This is because their **instinct** to hunt is still very strong but they are not hungry enough to eat the kill.

Sleeping

Your pet cat will enjoy sleeping somewhere warm, such as in the sun or near a radiator. Wild cats in hot places such as Africa will sleep during the day when it is hot and hunt in the evening or early morning when it is cooler.

◀ Pet cats (left) and wild cats like this tiger (below) spend most of their time sleeping, especially after a big meal.

Cubs and Kittens

Wild cat babies are called cubs. A baby pet cat is called a kitten. Wild and pet cats behave in a similar way when they are having their babies.

Giving Birth

Female lions are ready to have cubs when they are about 2 to 3 years old. Pet cats can have kittens when they are just 6 months old but it's better to wait until the female is about 2 years old before she has kittens. Both wild and pet cats will look for a quiet, safe place to have their babies.

▼ A lioness (below) will have two to four cubs in a litter; cats have three to eight kittens.

Life Cycle

A pet cat is pregnant for about 9 weeks. Newborn kittens are born with all their fur but they cannot see, hear, or stand up. They will drink their mother's milk until they are about 3 weeks old. This is called suckling. At about 3 weeks old, a kitten learns to walk and can see and hear. When the kitten is 6 weeks old it can run and will want to explore. At 10 to 12 weeks, a kitten is old enough to leave its mother.

1-week-old kitten

kittens suckling

4-week-old kitten

Caring for Their Young

When cubs and kittens are born, the mother will lick them clean. If the babies are in danger, the mother will carry them somewhere safe by picking them up in her mouth. Both wild and pet cats teach their young how to hunt.

▶ This cheetah is keeping her cubs clean by licking them.

Playing and Hunting

When your pet cat plays, it is using the same movements to catch its toy mouse that a lion uses to catch a deer or other prey in the wild.

Play Fighting

In the wild, big cats learn to hunt and look after themselves by watching their mother and by play fighting. Kittens also play fight. They chase each other and tumble and roll around but they do not hurt each other.

▶ Play fighting teaches kittens (above) and cubs (right) how to look after themselves and it also builds their confidence.

Stalking Prey

When wild cats are stalking prey, they crouch down low in the grass so they can't be seen. Your pet cat does the same thing when it is chasing a toy. The cat keeps its body low to the ground and creeps towards its prey. Then, when it is close enough, the cat springs forward to kill its prey.

PET POINT

Watch your pet using its hunting techniques when you play with it.

▼ The leopard (below) keeps its head low as its stalks its prey. The pet cat (right) crouches low down as it watches its toy roll through the grass. Both cats are getting ready to attack.

Making Their Mark

Both wild cats and pet cats have areas that are their **territory** that they mark to keep other cats away.

Scratching

Cats have **scent glands** in their paws so when they scratch, they leave a smell that tells other cats that this is their territory. The scratch marks also let other cats know that another cat lives here.

▶ Scratching helps to keep a cat's claws sharp as well as marking their territory. The tiger (right) scratches a tree and the pet cat (below) uses a scratching post.

Scratch 'n' Stretch

Some scientists believe scratching helps cats to stretch their muscles and get rid of stress. To stop your pet scratching the furniture never hit it or yell at it. Cover the place it scratches with plastic for a while to break the habit, and get a special scratching post or mat.

Making Their Mark

Cats also have scent glands on their head and at the base of their tail. So when a cat rubs up against you, a tree, or a piece of furniture, it is leaving its scent to mark its territory.

▼ This wild lynx (left) and pet cat (right) are both marking their territory.

Cat Talk

Cats make a lot of different noises, from a soft purr to a blood-curdling **yowl**. They also use their body to communicate.

Cat Noises

Cats make lots of different noises. Pet cats may hiss when they feel angry or threatened, purr when they are being stroked or petted, meow when they want to get your attention, and growl if they are unhappy or in pain. Wild cats mainly snarl, growl, and grunt. The big wild cats can roar.

▼ Cats in the wild, such as the puma (bottom), and pet cats (top), show their teeth and flatten their ears when they are scared or angry.

Purr-fect

Some cats purr a lot, others hardly ever do. Cats mostly purr when they are happy and content. However, they will also purr if they are in pain or scared. Some scientists believe that purring helps cats to stay calm if they are hurt and that it is a way of relaxing when stressed, but no one really knows.

▼ A tail held up in the air is a sign that a cat is pleased to see you.

Do It!

Listen to the sounds your cat makes and see how many different ones you can recognize. Does your cat make a certain sound when it wants to go out or be fed?

Tail Talk

Watch your cat's tail to see how it is feeling. A swishing tail means it is angry or wants to be left alone. When it walks towards you with its tail held high it is saying hello.

Instant Expert

All cats are part of the family *Felidae*. Wild cats live in most **habitats** around the world, from snowy mountains to scorching savannahs.

Where in the World

Wild cats are found in almost every region of the world except Australia and Antarctica. There are 40 species of wild cat including the tiger, lion, lynx, puma, leopard, jaguar, bobcat, ocelot, margay, and sand cat.

The Biggest...

The largest wild cats are tigers. The males are about 12 feet (3.6 m) long (nose to tail), stand about 3 feet (1 m) tall at the shoulder, and weigh up to 795 pounds (360 kg). The females are smaller.

The biggest domestic cat breeds are the maine coon and ragdoll (below). Maine coons can weigh up to 24 lb. (11 kg).

▼ Cats can look very different. The Devon rex (below) has very short fur and big ears. The ragdoll (far right) has a thick coat of fur and much smaller ears.

FAST FACT
Pet cats only make a meow noise with humans. Cats never meow at each other.

...and Smallest

There are many small wild cat species that are threatened because of hunting or habitat destruction. These include the kodkod found in South America that is thought to be one of the smallest wild cats. It is up to 30 in. (75 cm) long, about 8 in. (20 cm) tall and weighs about 5 lb. (2.2 kg).

Water Cats

Most cats prefer to avoid water, but in Asia, the wild fishing cat hunts for fish. It has webbed toes on its front paws and it taps the surface of the water to attract fish that it then snatches up. It will also dive into the water to catch fish.

The Turkish Van cat is a popular domestic breed that was first discovered living by Lake Van in Turkey. These cats enjoy playing with water and swimming. Many pet Van cats also enjoy a swim in the bath.

Pet Quiz

Now that you know a bit more about what is involved in caring for cats, is a cat the right pet for you?

1. When you go on vacation, what should you do with your pet?
  a) We'll put out lots of food for it.
  b) It'll be fine in the backyard until we get back.
  c) We will take it to a kennel.

2. How long can cats live?
  a) Not very long
  b) About 5 years
  c) About 15 to 20 years

3. What should you remember when you pick up your pet?
  a) Stroke it first
  b) Say its name
  c) Never squeeze it

4. If your cat holds its tail up straight, what does this mean?
  a) It's scared
  b) It's hungry
  c) It's happy to see you

5. What should you do if your cat scratches you?
  a) Put it outside
  b) Lock it in a room
  c) Say "no" and turn away

6. How much time do you have to spend with your pet each day?
  a) Not much. I'm very busy.
  b) I can spend lots of time with it on weekends.
  c) I'll spend some time with it every day.

Pet Quiz - Results

If you answered **(c)** to most of the questions then a cat could be for you.

Owning a Pet: Checklist

Think very carefully before you buy or take in a kitten. This pet could be with you for a very long time.

To be a good pet owner you should remember these five rules. Make sure your pet:

- never suffers from fear and distress
- is never hungry or thirsty
- never suffers discomfort
- is free from pain, injury, and disease
- has the freedom to show its normal behavior

This means that you have to make sure your pet has enough fresh water and food every day.

You must make sure there is somewhere warm and dry for your pet to take shelter if you leave it outside for a long period of time and it can't get indoors. Cats should never be left to live outdoors or be locked out over night.

Unless you want your pet to have kittens, all male and female cats should be neutered.

You must never hit your pet, shout at it or scare it, or leave it on its own for long periods of time. If it is sick or hurts itself you must take it to a vet immediately.

Microchipping

The best way to make sure your cat never gets lost is to microchip it. A microchip is a tiny object the size of a grain of rice that a vet inserts under the cat's skin. To identify the cat, a scanner is passed over the chip to get a number which is linked to your address.

Glossary

animal shelter a place where stray, unwanted, and injured animals can be taken and cared for before they are found a new home

breed a certain type of cat such as a Siamese or a Persian

camouflage fur color or coat pattern that helps the animal to blend in and hide in its surroundings

domesticated a cat that is tame and used to living with people

feral a domesticated cat that has turned wild because it has had to look after itself

groomed to be brushed or combed

habitats the types of places where animals live, such as a forest or in the desert

instinct a way of behaving that an animal is born with

litter a group of kittens all born at the same time to the same mother, also the material put in a cat's litter box.

litter box a plastic tray filled with special material that a cat uses as a toilet indoors

microchipped when a pet has a small electronic chip injected into its skin; the chip can be scanned to find out where the cat lives if it gets lost or has an accident.

mixed breed a cat that is not a purebred

neutered when an animal has had an operation so that it cannot breed

prey an animal that is hunted for food by another animal

purebred a cat bred from two cats of the same breed

scent glands a special skin gland found in certain areas of the body, such as the head, that leave a smell that can only be picked up by other animals

territory a particular place where an animal or group of animals lives

yowl a loud noise usually made as a warning or if an animal is in pain

Websites

Find a shelter where you can adopt a cat.
http://www.animalshelter.org/

Check out photos of pet cats in action!
http://kids.nationalgeographic.com/kids/photos/gallery/cats/

Care for your cat with these essential tips from the Humane Society.
http://www.humanesociety.org/animals/cats/tips/cat_care_essentials.html

Index